How to become a
FREELANCE
WRITER

I0005635

David Boyle

THE REAL PRESS
www.therealpress.co.uk

Published as print on demand and in various ebook formats in Great Britain in 2016 by the Real Press.

ISBN: 978-0955226380 (print)
ISBN: 987-0955226397 (ePUB)

Cover design by Hodge Creative Ltd.

For Judith and Andy

Introduction

I have been a self-employed writer now for nearly a quarter of a century. I am constantly being asked for advice by people, often those who have recently lost their jobs, about how they might go about it – what might be the best path or whether it was actually a good idea in the first place. I'm asked advice all the time by people, often early in their career, who have ended up freelance writing for want of anything else, or while they wait for precisely the right opening in the career of their dreams.

These are all valid questions, but I haven't really written this book for either of them. I wrote it primarily for people who have always dreamed of being self-employed writers as a career choice – but never quite dared to do it. I hope it helps them decide what to do and how. Forewarned, as they say, is forearmed.

I am aware of the hypocrisy about this. I never really planned to become a freelance writer myself. I was made redundant again by the television company I was working for, did a short couple of jobs to fill in time while I looked around, got a job, had the job abolished before I could take it up, and then suddenly found – lo and behold – I was self-employed. I can't even remember when I realised that was how I was going to stay. It seemed a perfect, though frenetic and often stressful existence. But it was free and it was independent in the most wonderful way. I adored it. I still do. I'm now well over fifty and unlikely ever to be offered another job, even if I wanted one, but I would politely turn it down – unless I felt it was only for a set period and something which perhaps only I could do.

Over the years, I've been so grateful to all those who have employed me. I tried keeping a list of all the companies I had carried out work for, but soon stopped trying. It doesn't run into hundreds but it very nearly does. I haven't loved working for all of them, exactly. One or two were a nightmare, but only one or two, and I've learned to hold onto the people I like. I've set out a little how I think that might be done in this book.

It isn't really a complete guide. I doesn't for example tell you anything much about how to write – I am assuming that is not a difficulty. It doesn't tell you everything. But it is also a tribute to all those other freelance writers, musicians, artists and creatives, struggling to squeeze a living out of a recalcitrant and intractable world. I must also warn you that it is based on my experience, such as it is – freelance writing in a wide variety of ways – but I would be the first to accept that there are other lessons, other ways of doing things

If you see things differently or have anything useful to add, do let me know...

I

Why freelance

Why on earth would anybody be a freelance writer? The pay is uncertain. The pension rights are non-existent. Freelance writing means constant rejection and disappointment, and rather a lot of unpaid negotiation. It means spending a great deal of time alone. It is precisely the kind of career path your parents warned you against and the school careers officer looked aghast when you first mentioned it.

So why do so many people think about doing it, especially at moments of crisis. Because they do. It can't just be the thought of sipping coffee in the Champs Elysées, armed with a notebook and huge literary ambition.

Probably the truth is a little more prosaic. It seems like the kind of life that many people tell themselves they want. And, let's face it, this is often the case when people feel a little battered by life, if they have been divorced or made redundant. Freelance writing seems like the kind of simple solution to the employment that suits people who don't want to deal with bosses too much – or maybe don't want to deal with people too much. It looks emotionally safe, if not quite financially safe.

This is, of course, about the worst reason for being a freelance writer, because it can be an excuse for not earning anything. Maybe even an excuse for not doing very much. It appears to be a justification for being alone with your own genius. Or your own hurt, of whatever kind.

Anyone who is determined be a self-employed writer really ought to start by looking closely at themselves to make sure this is not their motivation. Because this is not really an easy life. It does involve dealing with other people, sometimes with a great
deal of tact. It involves chutzpah and the ability to build trusting, long-term relationships. It isn't a place to hide for the walking wounded.

But I don't want to drive away my readers right at the beginning of the book. There are definitely attractions for the freelance writing life. My mother is always right about things, and she always told me that the most important thing in life is to find work you enjoy. I agree with her. It may not be the secret of life, but it is certainly one of the most important secrets. So if you love writing and communicating, and have a track record in doing so – and you have something to say – most writers, it seems to me, are hideously didactic, frustrated teachers – then it makes sense to pursue that kind of career.

The advantages

That is why you might want to write, but why do it for a living – and, above all, why be freelance? Well, the answer is that it isn't always the best way to be. Being your own boss is always a precarious business, but there are definite advantages. It means you have the freedom to plan when you work and when you don't. If you prefer working between 9pm and 3am, you can do so. I had a friend who was at his most productive between midnight and 2am and insisted on returning phone calls during those hours. When he finally got a job in an office, his bosses failed to understand why he arrived at work at lunchtime. Which was a pity, because he was brilliantly imaginative and highly effective, yet his employers could only see his absence in the mornings. He eventually despaired of their disapproval and disappeared, leaving behind a small box of chocolates.

Being freelance also means that you can break your work patterns if you want to. If you feel like a long walk after lunch, or prefer to just go to the seaside for the day, you can do so and nobody will mind. Nobody will even notice. Information technology also means that, if you want to take your laptop to the beach and work from there, then you can do that too – though probably not if you take the children.

The self-employed life is certainly good for family life. You can be there for the school nativity play and the obscure sports fixtures, if you want to be. You don't have to swap with anybody or get special permission. When the sun is shining, you can even get a whiff of the Paris dream. You can work in a cafe and imagine you are Hemingway in Madrid or Kerouac on the road. Philip Pullman wrote *Northern Lights* in the cafe at the Museum of Modern Art in Oxford. It can be done.

There have certainly been times in the past two decades – which is when I rather accidentally became self-employed – that I have blessed the day I was made redundant and given thanks that I had stumbled into this way of working. That is why it is also my responsibility to warn budding freelancers against the idea, especially if they are not really ready and don't have enough experience under their belt. But it would be wrong to deny that there are advantages, and they are enormous. That is the honest truth.

The disadvantages

Of course, there is an important other side to all this. The cafes you are forced to work in, to while away the time between appointments, are dull, draughty and lonely places without power points. Freelance writing can be a debilitatingly isolating business – though it doesn't always have to be (we will come onto that) – cut off from the companionship of colleagues and supportive friends. When it rains, it seems to just go on raining.

It is also makes you particularly prey to the two great paradoxes of the freelance life:

The Paradox of Enough

There can never be enough money, of course. There never is for anyone. We freelancers share that with practically everybody. It is one of the great mysteries of money that we would all be fine, no matter what our income is, if only we earned another ten per cent – but when we earn that extra ten per cent. The big problem for the freelancer is that the same also applies to paid work.

They say that being at war is a mixture between boredom and over-excitement. Being a freelance writer has elements of the same thing: you are always either too busy doing work or not nearly busy enough. But the real problem is that there is no happy medium between those two extremes. The Paradox of Enough suggests that life will always be one way or the other. Worse, the two seem to overlap in the middle, when there isn't enough money so you need to find more work but there isn't enough time to do it in. There is no escape. Freelance writing means, if you are going to succeed, that you will always be too busy. The only respite is that you can choose the hours in which you are busy in, and that is no small thing.

The Paradox of Vision

But there is another paradox about the freelance life. To survive freelancing writing in the long term requires one thing above all else. In the short term, other factors are more important, but this is about surviving for years rather than weeks. You need some vision of where you want to be and what you want to achieve – some vision of yourself. You need to know what are doing the whole thing for. But the problem with having any kind of vision – and especially one where you can really only rely on yourself to achieve it (you are your own career path) – is that it will bring with it constant and repeated disappointments.

There will be successes too, of course, but not nearly as many. There is one simple way of avoiding the disappointments, and that is not to have a vision or ambition about where you want to go, but then freelance writing becomes a mechanical business of earning money, without joy or direction, and it very quickly begins to lose its appeal. Therein lies the paradox.

Being a freelance writer inevitably means falling foul of both of these contradictions. There is no way of side-stepping them. Either or both are quite enough to make life seem dark and meaningless sometimes, particularly when you just seem to be slogging away writing things faster than they should be written. And let's face it, the one advantage that a freelance writer has, and which can earn you money in the real world, is the ability to complete a job faster than seems reasonable – and to charge for the reasonable time rather than the real time.

Self-reliance has other drawbacks too. It means that, if you get ill, you are economically vulnerable. Your health needs to be defended and that isn't always easy. Some creative people find that the very things that make them feel most alive can also make them ill. For years, I found that the act of putting one word after another could bring on eczema. It is an act of foolhardy self-belief to make yourself and your family quite so dependent, not just on your own skills, but also on your continuing health.

Of course, if you are thinking seriously of becoming a freelance writer, you may just have the necessary self-belief to do it. But that isn't axiomatic. If you are a pulsating mass of confidence, you may be powering away up the corporate career ladder, rather than looking for a space in your kitchen to open your laptop. As I mentioned before, some people opt for the freelance life just to avoid real life. You have to make sure that you are not one of those.

All this may be enough to prevent you leaping into the decision unwisely. It may even be enough to prevent you from reading further. I hope not. All I am saying is that the dreamy, imaginative side of freelance writing, like Hemingway or Kerouac, is not the whole story. Do it to chase a dream certainly – but don't do it to chase down the wrong dream.

A first checklist

So there you have it. Those are the benefits and drawbacks of freelance writing as a career, if there is such a thing. You parents may doubt it, and anyone with your best interests at heart may warn you against it. Your careers officer might stare at you goggle-eyed with incomprehension. The issue is, once you take this on, is how you can make some kind of career out of it – with rising income, status and satisfaction.

How do you know whether this is a sensible path to take for you? Well, this book will help you make up your mind, but this is my initial checklist:

1. Have you got at least five years of employed work behind you? Preferably ten?

2. Have you got some specialist knowledge? It doesn't matter what it is about.

3. Do you love finding out about things and communicating what you find? You do have to love it.

4. Do you aspire to some project or projects in the future and see yourself working towards that goal, whether it is a book, film or exhibition? It is no good simply to stand still.

5. Are you messianic about clear writing? Nothing else can drive you to enjoy re-writing some turgid official prose from lucrative employers.

6. Are you a self-starter? It is the tradition in mainstream journalism to leave deadlines until the very last moment. In freelance writing, this just leads to the most corrosive permanent stress.

7. Are you charming and reliable? No other combination will do if you want to be get more work from people. They must *want* to have you around again. You have to be the person you would most like to commission. Moodiness won't get you there.

8. Do you have relatively good health? At least, reliably predictable health? Because falling ill when you rely on yourself is a problem. If you have a family, it is potentially a disaster.

9. Are you relatively well-informed? You need to know enough about everything to know where to find out more, to know what the significance of things are, and much more besides.

10. Are you relatively happy? Or, if not, can you still manage to be reliable? Because if you are prone to debilitating depression, I don't think freelance writing is the solution, but then, I agree, neither is anything else.

If you can do all that, then – as Kipling might have said – you can be a freelance, my son/daughter. If you lack one of them, it might make sense to wait a while you sort it out. If you lack more than one, well, maybe think about something else. Don't stop writing, for goodness sake, but don't give up the day job just yet. Or the night job.

▌▌

What you need

Let us assume that you remain convinced that a life of freelance writing is the thing for you, despite all the drawbacks and warnings that I set out in the introduction. This chapter looks at what you will need to start. Of these the ten things I list in this chapter, the first two are by far the most important. There is no point in worrying about a desk or a bank account if you don't have clients. To believe otherwise is to suffer from one of the great scourges of freelance writing world – Detail Syndrome – where, through exhaustion, depression or addiction, you suddenly find that the details of a job, or the details of a new life, assume a huge importance compared to the thrust of the real thing what really matters.

Some years ago, I worked with a delightful colleague on a project to design a new kind of currency. This was a tough assignment with a number of conceptual problems at the heart of it, but the vast majority of his time was spent designing the membership card. Detail Syndrome; watch out for it. Guard against it, and especially when you are embarking on a new way of making a living.

In case you find it difficult to work out, and in case you were really worried about the shade your umbrella ought to be or the kind of pen you should wave at your notebook, these considerations are actually by far the most important.

#1. Get a main client

This is extremely important. Nobody should even consider giving up their life of regular employment for the uncertainty of freelance writing unless they have at least one major reliable and regular client. As a rule of thumb, one or both these three conditions must be met:

• One or more clients have agreed to provide you with enough work to cover about half your time for the foreseeable future.

• You have agreements for work that will cover the very basic costs of living.

Of course you will need more than one client. Otherwise, HM Revenue and Customs, in their wisdom, will say that you are not self-employed at all. But do not, whatever you do, resign your job if that one client is not firmly in place – even if that means working at night before you reach the stage when you can set up on your own.

Without that underpinning of your economic life, the first few months of freelancing will be full of desperate scrabbling around for work, and desperation is never the best attitude to get the regular work you need.

#2. Choose what to specialise in

The world is full of freelance writers. Many of them, it is true, are like freelance actors – they are actually doing something else and supplementing their income with the occasional flurry on the computer – but there is certainly competition out there. It is not enough just to be a writer. You stand a far better chance of getting work if you are also an *expert*.

It really doesn't matter what you are an expert in, or even if it is a clutch of different and varied sets of expertise, but there has to be something to give you an edge over all those generalists and journalists out there. Successful writers are specialists in something, and the narrower their specialism, the more likely they are to stand out.

It goes without saying that this expertise, though narrow, has to be interesting and relevant enough for somebody else to bother about – even if it is only *Caged Birds Monthly.*

The great thing about writing about something, anything almost as long as it is in print, is that people immediately start treating you like an expert, whether or not you actually know any more than they do. Writing an article about something with your name at the top is like a letter of qualification. Writing a book is *de facto* evidence of expertise and the world will beat a path to your door on the rare occasions that anyone wants to know about that subject.

For many years I have managed to scratch a partial living being an expert in the future of money. It isn't that I knew nothing about it; I knew quite a lot – and, which was perhaps more important, I came to know most of the people in the world with anything to say or do about complementary currencies. Though one of them complained at me being introduced as a speaker as an expert when, compared to him, I was nothing of the kind. He was right, of course.

I was also aware (and this is not as cynical as it sounds) that, when you are an expert in the *future* of something, nobody can disprove your assertions because they haven't had a chance to happen yet. For more than a decade I predicted the emergence of a multi-currency world, where we all use different kinds of money to underpin our lives. It hasn't happened yet, though I still maintain that it will (thank you; that will be £300 please...).

It also makes sense to have a battery full of different areas of expertise. It helps if these cross over – people like to categorise you in ways they can understand – but, frankly, life is too short to worry about things like that.

#3. Make a list of all the people you know who can help.

This is definitely a task you should do very early in the planning process. It is not an alternative to fixing up a stable employer for half your week – that has to be done before everything else – but it is what comes next. Writing lists of people is the first step towards organising work for the other half of your week.

I don't mean here that you should just include contacts who might be able to offer you work themselves. The net has to be cast much wider than that, to anyone who knows a lot of people, or who has contacts in the field you have chosen to write about, or who you knew in your career beforehand and liked you. You need to focus especially on what Malcolm Gladwell calls 'superconnectors' – people who know everybody. In his book *The Tipping Point*, he contrasts the impact made by Paul Revere riding through the night shouting "The British are coming!" Other people did it too, but had little impact; Paul Revere was a superconnector.

All those people need to know something about your plans, that you are available to work, what you want to do and when you start. It is probably worth going to see one or two of them as well, just to reinforce the point.

Once you tell them, and if you tell enough of the right ones, then the word should start to get around. And that is what you need if you are going to prize any kind of sustainable income from the jaws of a difficult world. Ideally, you should have a couple of other possible pieces of work at least discussed before you start. You need to be sure that, despite people's expansive rhetoric – which always promises more than it can deliver – there is more work available for you, if you are available to do it.

#4. Get advice

This goes with the previous requirement. Letting it be known among your contacts, friends and former colleagues, that you are setting out on your own is also a process of getting advice. You need to ask them as well as tell them. Where might you find work? What might you offer? How should you pitch yourself? Is this really a good idea right now? All these are important questions – but there is another one too, if you have the nerve to ask it. Can I hack it? Do you really think, honestly, that this is a good idea? If not, what do you suggest instead?

It makes sense to ask people you respect, who have some reason to know the market – but also people you think will give you a genuinely honest answer. Then, of course, you have to listen, even – in fact especially – when their advice contradicts what you have been telling yourself.

You then have to act on it, or at least gather together the common threads and act on them. The problem with asking advice is that, all too often, it comes out conflicting. On the other hand, it is easy to persuade yourself that the advice is conflicting when actually there are a number of points which do seem to crop up regularly – if you are honest with yourself.

You do have to be honest with yourself in this game. Delusions do not lead to a sustainable income and, often, reading a text you have been asked to edit or re-write involves being honest first with yourself about your reactions to it.

#5. Find somewhere you can work

Renting office space is really not a good idea at this stage, but you do need to think about the two or three main things that you used to get from an old-fashioned office. A desk with a computer, some company and somewhere to make tea and coffee – all absolutely vital.

Let's deal with the company problem first, because freelance writing can be staggeringly isolating if you are not careful. Perhaps there are neighbours planning something similar, or friends in the vicinity where you can schedule a weekly meeting or even a daily coffee, preferably people who can boost your ego or soothe your ruffled feathers when things are going badly. I know some writers who use Twitter to replace the jaunty cut and thrust of office life, but that has never been enough for me. I need to work in an office at least a day a week. Or failing that, I need a great deal of café breaks with friends.

I don't think you can avoid this. Isolation makes for depression, and you can't really be a freelance writer from under the duvet. It is true that Winston Churchill dictated most of his articles from his bed, but most of us are not Churchillian enough for that, and he famously had to battle his Black Dog depression too.

Then there is the question of where you are going to put your computer. The front room is probably not a good idea, unless you want your life completely dominated by your work. For my first decade or so of freelancing, I made this mistake. In fact, I spent 11 September 2001 watching the World Trade Centre in flames as I wrote a chapter of a book on authenticity, because of my unhealthy habit of working while BBC News 24 was on at the same time. In fact, I had been hoping to watch Laurence Olivier as Nelson and Vivian Leigh as Lady Hamilton on the other side. Either way, I don't recommend it.

No, find another corner somewhere where you can go and work, a tiny bedroom, even a cupboard, anywhere you can actually slog away unambiguously. Then, when you believe you need a coffee break, you can allow yourself a glimpse at the news channels or the Twitter feed.

#6. Get insurance

The main legal threat to freelance writers is probably libel. There is a real risk that, through no obvious fault of your own, you may write something which you only realise is defamatory because the person describes reacts to it that way. Often it is your fault, but it is just such a tiny mistake – a small error in checking, an unfortunate juxtaposition of words – yet it still leads to this kind of disaster.

The trouble is that libel insurance is ruinously expensive, especially for something that – unless you are working on gossip columns – you will almost certainly never need. You can reassure yourself that most companies will not sue if it will just cost them money, as it will suing an individual. But you can't be sure. On the other hand, there are some reasonable office insurance packages which include third party liability, and which will insure your office equipment when it is ambiguous whether they are covered on the household insurance.

There are, in fact, specific insurance packages around designed for writers and these may be worth thinking about:

Public liability insurance. This is usually required for giving talks in schools, which is something many writers have to do, and some even like to do. The National Association of Writers in Education offers free public liability insurance if you join them (www.nawe.co.uk).

Professional indemnity insurance. Sometimes this includes libel, sometimes not, but it is expensive anyway. Packages normally include negligence, unintentional infringement of copyright, unintentional breaches of confidentiality, loss of documents, liability to others including damage to property or injury. It is expensive but it may keep your mind at rest and both the National Union of Journalists and the Society of Authors offer schemes through their membership.

Office insurance. This may be worth taking out if only because, if you are using your home as an office, it can sometimes be ambiguous whether your office equipment will be covered under your contents insurance.

Tax protection insurance. It is well known that investigations by the Revenue & Customs are pretty rare, but can turn everything upside down if you are unfortunate to incur one. You can now get legal expenses insurance against such an eventuality, and it doesn't cost very much.

#7. Get a website

Or a Facebook page devoted to your work. Or two, of course. It need not be expensive or overly designed. There are off the peg websites in many different software packages including Word. There are free blog designs on Google or Wordpress or others. It may be that you can wait for the blog, but you need something which is an online calling card, where you can publish some of your work, and where you can announce and link to the specialisms that will get you work. It is worth doing, believe me.

#8. Register as self-employed

The sooner you can sort out these details with HM Revenue and Customs, the better. You will be paying two kinds of National Insurance yourself, and it is relatively easy to organise this – once the tax authorities accept that you are genuinely self-employed. In fact this is usually the main delay. You will need to demonstrate that you have a range of different employers, otherwise you will have to go on stuck inside PAYE at your main employment, and declaring the other earnings on a tax return, until such time as they can be convinced.

This is a pain in the neck, but employers are terrified of accepting that you are self-employed and then being landed with having to pay your national insurance and other costs at a later date.

They are also often terrified of falling foul of immigration legislation which means that even temporary employment may involve showing your passport. This is tyrannical and deeply irritating but, for the time being – our tickbox culture being what it is – we have to put up with it.

#9. Get a tax account

This is so important that I am going to cover it properly later. Freelancers must pay income tax on what they earn like everyone else, and are usually expected to do so twice a year, at the end of July and at the end of January. The trouble is, for many of us, that we have long since spent the money that we owe in tax, and tax returns are occasions for great panic and misery as we desperately work out how to pay.

There are two ways to avoid this. The first is to subsume your work under the auspices of a limited company, and to pay yourself using PAYE. This may or may not be a good idea later, but it is probably too expensive and onerous while you are finding your feet as a freelancer. There are other issues around paying VAT which are beyond the scope of this book.

The other way to avoid the angst is to combine great determination, great fortitude of mind and a tax account, so that the money you anticipate paying in income tax goes straight into an account earning interest until such a time as the taxman demands it. This is difficult to do at first, but is absolutely vital and it has some unexpected added benefits, as I will explain later.

Done all that? Right, then it is time to begin.

But, hold on a moment. Before you jump right in, there is one other area to think about. I have deliberately not included in this book instructions about how to write for different audiences. I am assuming that nobody in their right mind would consider becoming a freelance writer unless they were already pretty proficient and confident when it comes to writing, and I take no responsibility for those not in their right mind.

On the other hand, it is worth thinking about what makes you an effective writer. Practice is absolutely vital, of course. I have already quoted the bestselling science writer Malcolm Gladwell, and I do so again: he suggests that it takes 10,000 hours – about ten years work – to become a master of a craft. Every piece of work you do improves your abilities for the next one. Listening to good writing of various kinds is a very good way of practicing too. In fact, I believe I was able to write effectively largely because of an unhealthy habit of listening to BBC Radio 4 too much at a very early age. I felt I could hear the way it should be in my head,

We also need to rid ourselves of some of those writing ticks that you get from too expensive an education. You can always tell those with classical training because of their awkward sentence constructions – Caesar, having conquered Gaul... and so on. Worse, you can usually tell the university educated writers by their constant reputation of awkward words like 'nevertheless' and 'however', which students learn to scatter liberally through their essays to make it seem as if there is some kind of argument there.

I believe that the task of a freelance writer, the mission if you like, is to make things interesting, clear and easy to read, and that means simplicity above everything else. Simplicity because that means clarity. It means not rendering prose into some kind of camp jargon, or worse – officialese, but into something that people might actually say.

That may be too prosaic, as they say, for some. But it is an important task, even if it isn't a very exclusive or self-important one. Freelance writers nurture and protect the language. They excise meaningless buzzwords. In fact, I have occasionally found – working for charities in particular – that, once you have stripped away the jargon, nothing whatever has happened after all. It is a salutary experience, to be asked to re-write something about nothing, but that is our calling.

The lesson is that practice makes perfect. If someone is prepared to train you a little more, all well and good – and there are certainly skills which freelance writers need which it is useful to be trained in, like public speaking. But generally, you need to know about writing already if you are going to survive like this.

There is one exception to this rule, and I recommend this for anyone starting out as a freelance writer. Good writing is always creative. The task of finding the right words and phrases is hardly different from the daily job of a novelist or poet, even if the results are more ordinary and deliberately so. I found that learning creative writing made an enormous difference to the imagination and flexibility that I was able to bring to very ordinary projects.

Every Friday evening, I would gather with others around my friend Carol's kitchen table in Camden, for an institution known as Writing Space, and learn to write more creatively. I hadn't expected this to feed through into my other work, but it did and amazingly so. It also, of course, allowed me to branch out into more creative areas of writing myself.

So I don't want to be pompous about the writer's calling. It is very mundane really, though very necessary, but conversely it can be hugely improved by learning to be creative. And one of the problems of about being self-employed is that, not only are you responsible for you own career development, you are also responsible for your own own in-house training.

▮▮▮

Selling yourself

The very words 'selling' and 'yourself' are enough to strike fear into the hearts of most of us, when they are heard next door to each other. In fact, the thought that perhaps we might have to do this one day is enough to put some people off self-employment for life. We are on the receiving end of such a stream of brutish and useless attempts to sell us goods or services, every day – in fact one estimate suggests that we are prey to 10,000 advertisements between every dawn and dusk. It is hardly surprising that we react against the whole idea.

The good news is that, for being a freelance writer, brutish advertising really isn't necessary. Of course there are going to be difficult and embarrassing phone calls – offering articles to harassed editors, suggesting new work to people you hardly know – some of that is going to be inevitable. But you don't have to provide some kind of hard sell day in, day out. Being a successful freelance writer does not mean you have to press your claims fervently and embarrassingly on difficult potential employers. It doesn't have to be like that.

Of course, if you're good at it, and self-effacing or charming enough, then a little push can go a long way. The point here, as I shall explain in this chapter, is that it isn't necessary.

Specialisation

The key to selling yourself effectively, as I hinted in the last chapter, is specialisation. I don't know how many freelance writers there are out there. Tens of thousands in the UK alone, possibly more. Some of them will undoubtedly be better than you are, more experienced and better connected. When you start out, it really is not going to be feasible to compete with all the others. You need to even up the odds a little.

The way to do this is to specialise. It doesn't have to be a specialisation in just one area, though it helps if there is some connection between your various areas of expertise – otherwise it can be confusing for people who don't know you. By all means specialise in two or three distinct areas, but once it goes beyond that there can seem to be a hint of insanity about it, at least from a distance. Worse, people may not believe your expertise goes very deep.

But one thing your choice of expertise absolutely must have is *authenticity*. It has to be real. This has to be an area you are genuinely passionate about or fascinated by and determined to make some kind of contribution to, even if that contribution is initially the need to explain to people what it is all about in clear language – and if there is one skill you need as a freelance writer, then it is the ability to express something clearly and interestingly, preferably also engagingly. But that is a different topic.

Once you have this expertise, then there is at least an overwhelming reason why you might be commissioned to write an article, or edit something, above someone else who is far more experienced than you are. Once you have written one thing, then the proof of your expertise is there for all to see. If you can manage to write a book or even a short pamphlet on the subject, that is expertise by definition and, if you play it right, the world will beat a path to your door.

But I repeat the most important point about authenticity. Don't whatever you do choose an area of expertise because you think the market is there. Choose something that excites you and, and you will find there will be an energy about what you do that draws people to you. If the energy isn't there, you might as well not bother.

Which brings me to a related point. The market is doubly irrelevant here, as long as there is some interest or relevance in what you are excited about. The narrower your expertise, then the more certain you are to get the work once a potential client tracks you down. This is the new economics of micro-producing. In the early years of the print-on-demand website Lulu, their bestselling title was about an extremely rare breed of dog. It was the only book that had ever been devoted to this breed. As a result, anyone with an interest in those particular dogs – and there were few of them – bought the book. They didn't buy a generic book about dogs. They bought that one. The narrower the market, the clearer the niche.

I would like to be able to say that I worked all this out for myself and applied it to my own career, but I can't say that is true. On the other hand, I believe I unwittingly did something along these lines. As a newspaper reporter in the 1980s, I became excited by the emerging green movement and reported on it in Oxford whenever I managed to smuggle something past the editor. Inevitably, that meant I found myself writing about planning a great deal. For my next job, I managed to fall into the role of editor of a magazine about planning and found that I absolutely loved it.

This was a little strange since planning is the meeting point of geography and economics. I had never studied economics and I gave up geography at the age of thirteen. It would have been an understatement to say that I was under-qualified for the job. If I had been older than twenty-seven, perhaps I would have thought twice about expressing my opinions on a subject I knew so little about in my own columns in the magazine. But I went right ahead and, would you believe it, people responded.

I found myself at the end of that period fascinated by the emerging topic of green economics, which is how I came to work for the first time for the New Economics Foundation. It was the period of the The Other Economic Summit conferences in London, and this seemed to me to be where the energy was. I wrote about green economics wherever I could. It was a niche subject compared to the broader green movement, but it suited me.

A few years later I found myself specialising even further, because I became excited by the idea of green money. I discovered green dollars on a visit to New Zealand in 1991 and was absolutely thrilled by the idea that people could simply create their own currencies. I wrote a book. People behaved to me as if I was an expert and so, by then and in a narrow sense, I was.

All those specialisations have paid off in terms of commissions. And every time I specialised further, I did not leave the old expertise behind. Yet, every time also, the new expertise made me distinctive and therefore employable as a writer or editor.

So perhaps, when you sit down and start to think about how to make yourself employable as a freelance, the first task is to make an audit of what thrills you most – not just what you know, but what you might know, what you could bear to know in the future.

What work to do

Here the advice is the opposite of what I said above. If it makes sense, for good marketing reasons, to specialise, the opposite is true when it comes to thinking about precisely the kind of work you need to be prepared to do. You are a freelance writer, of course, so it makes sense that it needs to be involved with words. Basic writing, articles, features, books, comments, blogs, websites will all be part of your stock in trade. But don't confine yourself to that. Editing needs to be part of your battery of weapons as well. So does the business of re-writing, and – since you are an expert – broadcasting and speaking. In fact, speaking – if people believe you have something to say – is always going to be more lucrative than writing. Writers are always regarded just a little as hacks; speakers never are. That is quite unfair but still the case.

In any case, it is absolutely astonishing how much re-writing needs to be done. It helps to be a freelance writer if you have a deep sense of mission about banishing bad writing from the world. I don't mean ungrammatical writing. Some people mind about that; it doesn't bother me perhaps as much as it should. But unclear, dull, bureaucratic writing, borrowing the legal language from generations gone by, sends me mad with frustration. So I never looked on re-writing jobs as somehow beneath me – which is a good thing, because otherwise I would have starved. I regard them as a small part of the crusade against gobbledegook everywhere.

Perhaps we writers should be grateful that there are such incompetent people writing copy out there, because it provides us with an underpinning to our living. In fact, most people are perfectly good at expressing themselves. They just lack the confidence to do it on the page for all to see.

We hacks have little in our favour. They can disapprove of what we have written and never ask us again. They can fail to pay us properly or in full, and frequently do, but we have two great advantages when it comes to freelance writing, and they both derive from the same thing: they don't really understand writing. They overcomplicate it. It might as well be plumbing for your average managing director.

Advantage #1. They don't know how long it takes.

As a surviving freelance writer you need to be able to work faster than anyone thinks possible, so that you can sell your time a couple of times over. More on this later. Of course, this can hardly apply when you are working in their office, but oddly enough I find I can work even faster in someone else's office – where I am unlikely to get the urge to make myself toast or to suddenly do the hoovering, and where people are less likely to phone me.

Advantage #2. They don' think they can do it themselves.

I remember being asked to write the managing director's editorial column to go on the front of a company newsletter I had been commissioned to write. This was a grand newsletter; not the usual kind which are lineally related to *Pravda* in their commitment to truth and imagination, but a genuinely forward-thinking and an innovative read. The managing director was the inspiration for much of this, but he told me he could not write.

We met over breakfast in a cafe around the corner from his office, and he told me generally what he wanted to say. I recorded the conversation. When I got back home and listened to the tape, I found that he had been so lucid that all I really needed to do was to transcribe what he said and tidy it up a little. That is what I did. To my surprise, the managing director was absolutely delighted with it. He added: "You see, I just can't do that kind of thing."

His ignorance of his own competence, and so many like him, allows freelance writers to make a living. That is why it makes sense, incidentally, not just to rely on journalism – which is capricious, badly-paid and time-consuming – but to spread the net much further to include anything to do with words.

But why stop there? If you specialise as I suggested above, then you will find yourself valued not just for your ability to communicate, but also for your knowledge. And when it comes to adding value, they will pay you for your knowledge much more happily. The logical extension of that is that people will also eventually pay you for your advice. It may be written down, but it isn't your words or your skills as a wordsmith they are after, it is the contents of the words. You may even be employed to put some of those ideas into practice. And in this way we might just scrape out a sustainable income into old age.

This is not compromising with our vocation as writers. Far from it. It is one of the paradoxes of freelance writing that – and all careers come to this – the more successful you are at it, the less you find yourself doing the nitty-gritty that you are actually so good at. Freelance writing is like casting yourself into the river and seeing where it leads. It is about taking opportunities when they come up. And, despite being a wonderful life, it does have to be said that freelance writing is not as well paid as, say, consultancy.

Consultancy, as Arthur Daley used to put it, "nice little earner".

Marketing

I said that hard-selling was unnecessary. It may even be counter-productive. In my experience, most people who commission us are looking for someone they trust and someone they get on with. They may be put off by too intensive a selling job. We freelance writers have to be cleverer than that.

The clue is in the business of specialisation. When you specialize, it narrows the field of possible employers – that is, of course, the disadvantage – but it does mean that you know who you need to cultivate. Find out who you know who has contacts there. Get to know them. Meet them at conferences. Talk to them about what interests you, in the hope that it might also interest them. But I believe the effective marketing of yourself means that there need not be a constant offer. What there does need to be is a quiet sense of confidence, a sense of expertise and a sense of passion. And, of course, a safe pair of hands (or set of fingers).

That means that you are not so much advertising what you can do. You are simply telling anyone who is interested what you are interested in – and what you are working on, what thrills you and why it's important. That is why your own passion for your specialist subject or subjects is absolutely vital. Because it is infectious and says more about you than any amount of ordinary marketing .

It is the same if you have a website or a blog. The atmosphere should be not so much about what you can do for people. The fact that you are open for business is not the most important message. It helps sometimes if they wonder whether you really *are* available. The message is: this is what excites me. This is what I have been writing. This is what I am working on and this is what fascinates me at the moment.

The website needs to be a showcase of your passion and only incidentally a showcase of your writing ability. Of course it needs to be that too, but by implication rather than up front. The same applies to your blog. It is you and your passion that is on show, and that is the way it should be.

As far as marketing is concerned, there are more opinions about it than there are marketers. It will depend precisely what subjects you have chosen to specialise in. There will undoubtedly be areas where this does not apply. But there is no area of writing where the basic rule does not apply: find out who the people are who might commission you. Find out who knows them and cultivate them. Not necessarily for the purpose of immediate work but because – one day – they will need you. And it makes sense for them to know where you are.

Pricing

Knowing what to charge seems like a nightmarish question at the outset and it always is something of a problem. To most normal people, the thought of looking someone in the eye and demanding money is a daunting prospect, especially if it is for you rather than for some organisational entity you represent.

Americans tend to imbibe the confidence they need with their mother's milk. A friend of mine who commissioned articles for a women's magazine told me about one encounter with an American writer who introduced the subject with this immortal sentence: "Honey, I don't even take the cover off my computer for less than $1,000". It may be that it is a peculiarly British trait to be embarrassed by money, but we rarely get anything in our education that allows us to put on that kind of front.

The first problem is to set a day rate, or at least some means of beginning to ask a daunting question, as I have been asked, like: "Can you talk me through your charging structure?" I am not going to suggest one here because it will date the book but the thing to do is to ask friends in the same business what they charge per day. Bear in mind that it needs to amount to a living wage, and though it might feel uncomfortable asking for this at first, a day rate is a good building block for working out what to charge.

It also means that you begin to relate what you are charging to the time it will take you, which is a good start. I know that National Union of Journalists and the Society of Authors collect contemporary amounts that are paid for articles or readings, and these are useful guides to keep. But you need a regular day rate, because it is the basis for everything else.

So here is my advice about what you might say when someone asks what you will charge for a job:

1. Say nothing to start with.

2. Say you will work it out and get back to them the following day.

3.   Ask around for any similar experience, but – if there isn't any – and there usually isn't...

4.   Try and work out how long the job would take a normal human being (not you; you will do it faster) in days and half days – a reasonable time for the job and see what that would come out as.

5.   Add in expenses and travelling time.

6.   Ask yourself: what do they expect to pay?

7.   Split the difference. I know that may mean you will be earning less than you think they might actually pay, but this may sometimes be an advantage to start with. When you know them better, they will be more open to negotiation if it turns out to be too little.

8.   Run through a little list of your own of expensive pitfalls you might have to work around. Will you have to work from their office? Will you have to oversee their complex and laborious signing off process? Will you be involved in a whole series of exhausting liaison meetings to keep their bosses happy, which will actually take much longer than then work itself? Will you have to do it twice

because they haven't been clear about what they want and you haven't asked?

9.   Suggest your figure very tentatively and say you can negotiate if necessary – you don't want to lose the job because you have misunderstood.

10. If they say yes, point out that this won't include your list of expensive pitfalls. Politely of course. Suggest you have another think when the first phase is over – or that you might have to 'revisit' that if there is a long sign-off process, but that of course you will get it into a position where they are happy. This is ambiguous but it gives you wriggle room if something goes wrong.

11. If they say it isn't quite what they expect, try negotiating on time not money – say you might be able to do it in fewer days, if certain conditions apply, and as long as the pitfalls don't happen. You need a way of making sure they don't think you made up the figure quite as you did.

12. If they still say no, well, it depends how much you want or need the job.

This is certainly not the way you are supposed to negotiate. I set it out here because it is the way I do it, and it is worth remembering that you both have to feel good about the price, if this is going to be the beginning of a happy, long-term relationship. I have certainly charged too little in my time. I have also charged too much once or twice, but always because – through my fault or theirs – I have misunderstood the unspoken rules of our business relationship. I have only once ever fallen out with a client and that was because they thought I was being outrageously greedy, when I thought I was following their instructions. It just goes to show – and a number of things: that a sustainable income depends on sustainable relationships, and those depend on good communication. They also depend on the writer's continuous assessment of what the other side expects.

And here is one of the secrets of the freelance writer's life, as I hinted earlier. We manage to pay our way, as writers, despite the traditionally low payments for journalism or book writing, because we know we can finish a job much faster than most people in the outside world realise. That is a great advantage and a secret that must be laboriously defended. It means we can potentially sell the same time twice over. So what you need to calculate in this initial negotiation is not just how long it will take you to do, but also how long an editor or manager might reasonably *expect* you to take – and to charge accordingly.

I have warned against charging too much. It also never makes sense to set your charges too low. It may well seem that you will win yourself more work, and – within reason you might – but beyond that, then this is a fantasy that comes from listening to too many economists. The truth is that, if you charge too little, most potential employers will discount you. They certainly want a bargain, but not at the risk of employing someone who does not rate themselves very highly.

I learned this lesson myself the hard way, having been asked to come in and chat with the manager of a consultancy I very much admired. "What is your day rate?" he asked. I had just started out and quoted something extremely low, having not prepared myself for this obvious question. I could see the look of shock on his face. I never heard from him again.

More on negotiation

This might imply that there is no place for healthy negotiation, which is of course not true. There are business manuals out there which suggest that you avoid it, but the truth of the matter is that I negotiate all the time – especially when I am charging for speaking engagements, because I know that the budgets available to the people employing me vary very widely indeed.

Speaking engagements are notoriously difficult to price. There is the preparation time, the travel time, maybe even an overnight stay, so there is rather a lot of scope for negotiation. I usually say what I normally charge (about a day and a half) but say that I can negotiate. They normally come back with a reasonable offer. There may also be times, especially when you are promoting something, when it makes sense to speak for nothing except expenses, but that is another story.

This is no doubt very unprofessional of me, but I have an idea of in my mind of the life I want. It involves dealing with clients where I have the kind of relationship of trust where they urge more money on me and I offer to do it for less. That is the kind of relationship I want – though you will find it in none of the business manuals. It means a different and more relaxed way of going about things, open about the possibilities and about what can be negotiated and what can't.

Andrew Ferguson, the founder of the innovative Breakthrough Centre, used to urge us members to negotiate only about the amount of time a job will take – and to leave the day rate sacrosanct. This is the approach I suggested under the heading of negotiation. It isn't always possible, but it is a trick which has allowed me to take jobs where the employer could never have afforded me otherwise. I stick to the day rate but say that I can probably complete most of the work – or a little less than what they want – in half the time, knowing that I can actually do it still faster than that.

The other time it seems to me when they require some kind of negotiation downwards is when you are offered a long-term contract and where circumstances make it sensible to negotiate. Because regular work is what we all need as freelancers.

But beware the other end of the scale. There must be a minimum below which you will not go. Some book packagers and small publishers can provide a reasonable living for freelance writers who can write books extremely fast. But some of them pay less than it seems reasonable even then, and in those circumstances, very reluctantly, you have to know when to say no. Especially if you are being given a contract where you get no continuing rights or royalties.

I find myself constantly irritated by the academic world. Universities are notoriously bureaucratic and difficult when it comes to paying (it makes sense to hammer out details of how you will be paid before you actually do work for them). As for academic publishers, they expect you to write for next to nothing – and sometimes nothing – and also to indemnify them against various legal actions. And often they won't even give you a copy. My advice is this: do the work if you like, but don't sign the contract. Or, if you do, strike out the bits you don't like and initial them. They rarely seem to notice.

IV

Dealing with clients

I hinted in the last section that I have a heretical view on this, but I commend it to anyone who wants to be self-employed. My fulfilment in my work, and my relaxation levels and the sheer fun I have at work, are going to be hugely enhanced if I can work for friends than if I work for people I don't know, don't like or don't trust. Most of my friends are never going to employ me so it follows that I must, if I possibly can, be friends with the people I work with and work for.

Put like that, it is rather obvious. Of course it may never be possible for all my clients to be friends, but that is the objective. There are disadvantages to this, of course. You can't find yourself paid much more than you are worth by people who know you well. You can't pull the wool over their eyes or deceive them about what other people pay. You can't in fact be paid as well by friends as you can by those who barely know you. On the other hand, they are a good deal more reliable, in terms of payment and far more understanding if you run into any kind of difficulties. They will also, hopefully, employ you again and again. But they will only do that if they trust you and enjoy working with you. Both have to work, and consistently so.

That is why I would prefer to have conversations where I beat my own price down and they urge me to raise it – because we know and trust each other, and care about each other – than I would to have the kind of usual kind of negotiation which goes the other way. Even if I was to earn more that way.

If this is unprofessional and unbusinesslike of me, then so be it. That is how I prefer to live. I also believe that, in the long run, I will be better off financially as a result. But there is another disadvantage as well, which I will return to later. If you are too successful at this strategy, and the line has become hopelessly blurred between your friends and your clients, then when do you ever escape from work? But that is a more fundamental problem and I will deal with it in the last section.

Finding clients

There are a few common elements about getting work across the genres and the first, and most obvious, flies in the face of the world we may hope is out there. It is that it doesn't matter *what* you know compared to how much it matters *who* you know. But don't despair: being a freelance writer requires a certain dose of *chutzpah.* It may involve generating *chutzpah* when you don't really feel it, but then that is a common problem for anyone who is self-employed.

The only comforting aspect is that the people you need to know are almost certainly immune to the hard sell, so that would hardly work even if you could manage it. This is where your specialist knowledge is important. Share what it is you're interested in at the moment, start a blog, use social media, get involved with other people interested in the same things.

Which brings us to the second common feature. The need to have a great deal more basic intelligence about who you need to know in the publications or organisations, or in the subject areas, that excite you the most. Who are they? Who do they know? And most important – what problems do they have, what gaps that you might be able to fill? This kind of information you may have to find out just by asking them in a roundabout way. Find some way to start a dialogue, be useful, offer help – maybe even unpaid help to start with, but don't beg for favours: offer them instead. Of course, it may be a favour if they try you out, but it needs to be a reciprocal one.

Beyond that, there are a number of different areas where you might think about finding work, and don't stick to just one of them:

Newspapers
Read the bylines. Find out who covers your areas of interest. Look online to find out who commissions articles in those sections, and work out what kind of stories they need – if it can be covered by a staffer, it probably will be: you need to bring in something they don't have already. Start small; be useful.

Magazines
The same applies to magazines. You need to know who commissions and what you might bring that works well for them, yet would not be something they might cover using their usual suspects. Find out when their deadlines are – pitch by email and then follow-up at the least stressful moment by phone. Understand they are likely to be very busy. If they're not interested straight away, they are unlikely to be persuaded otherwise.

Broadcasting
This is more difficult, because you need to know the intermediaries who make the television and radio programmes. They will be on the look out for programme

ideas, and don't assume they will be saints. You need to be so crucial to the story that, even when they get the budget, they can't cut you out of the loop.

Think tanks

Think tanks need researchers and writers, though it helps to have an economics degree or some kind of research qualification. They will also need project ideas, though again – if they have to do all the fundraising – then you may not be as useful in the project as you might hope, Either way, it is important to know beforehand which think tanks work in your area of expertise and who runs those departments.

Websites

There are of course crowdfunding websites which can fund work as a writer, like Unbound or Byline, but you may need something of a track record and possibly also a support group to do this. There are also opportunities to write for websites, but generally speaking – like so much of the online publishing world – they haven't really factored in the costs of paying for content. This is definitely shortsighted, and may not last – who wants to read endlessly recycled words after all? – but it is still the case at the moment. You can also build up enough of an online presence with your own blog that you may either make money from advertising or from selling products. These are not mutually exclusive either, and there are plenty of guides – by people claiming to make huge sums every month – so it is pointless to repeat it here.

Books

Ebooks and conventional books appear to be evolving in different directions. Both provide opportunities for writers but advances are in seriously short supply. Since academics will virtually pay publishers to publish their work, then content is always available to them. But the basic rules are the same. Find out which agents cover your area of interest, which publishers and which editors (see who your closest authors thank in their acknowledgements) and come up with a proposal. A proposal is, as I have often been told, the book you want to write in microcosm. Don't send it off hopefully with a covering letter to someone you haven't ever spoken to, and be prepared anyway for a healthy dose of rejection to start with.

Or have a go at self-publishing. Start by checking out Createspace.com and see what you think, but don't assume that the money will just flow in – self-publishing is so exhausting that you have to enjoy it for its own sake. Or alternatively, get to know which book packagers work in your area of knowledge and offer them help.

Making friends

This heading implies a great deal about your basic strategy when it comes to dealing with clients. You must be friendly. Remember their names, a very basic requirement and – if you are anything like me – you will need techniques for doing this. Maybe even their remember their birthdays (Anita Roddick used to say she realised her company had reached a new level when she didn't know the names of her employees' pets). Be pleased to see them – and there should be no need to pretend: if you are not pleased to see them, you would probably be happier working for somebody else. Enjoy your conversations with them. Be interested in them as people. Think about the conundrums they face and the extent to which you can help. Trust them when it counts.

Do all these things and, magically, you will find they do the same to you.

None of this suggests that you should be anything less than professional. You have to do a good job and on time, otherwise they will not employ you again, however much they might like you. Part of the trust requires that you meet their deadlines – the deadlines you agreed with them at the start of the project. That is absolutely vital. Being a freelance writer is not about living in a garret, drinking too much and missing deadlines. It isn't even about staying up all night before the deadline as if this was some kind of student essay crisis. The deadline must be met, comfortably, preferably with time to spare and certainly with time for checking. My worst fault as a freelance writer is that I hate checking. I have to force myself to do it, aware that clients assume that, if there are spelling mistakes – even if you warn them that it isn't finished – then they will think you have bodged the work.

There are three absolutely vital aspects to dealing with clients, and they apply to absolutely every job. If you can do these, you will succeed. If not, you will struggle as a freelance writer. They are:

1.   Meet the deadline, with time to spare.

2.   Exceed their expectation in some way, even if it is just some extra information which you can make available to them. You need to consider at the start of every task how this might be possible.

3.   Be charming.

Do all three of those consistently and you will have a long career as a freelance writer. It will also be fulfilling.

Planning a job

The whole business of making money out of writing, not to mention hitting that all important deadline, really depends so much on being able to judge how long each job will take you. As I said before in the last section, there are really two judgements to be made here and both of them are vital to pricing jobs – first, how long it will take you and, second, how long they *believe* it should take you. They will say they don't know – and of course the truth of the matter is neither do you – but they will still have a sense of it. They will have a figure in their mind above which they will not want to go, and below which will make them suspicious that you have misunderstood.

The question of how long a job will take you depends very much on you having an accurate sense of your own capabilities and what you can and can't achieve. I have to say I find this one of the most difficult aspects of freelance writing. I endlessly underestimate time, whether it is how long a journey will take or how long a job will take. This business of judging how long projects will take you is therefore not so much a technical matter – though clearly it is also that – but a matter of self-knowledge.

Here is one way of planning ahead. If a working day is about eight hours, less an hour for a break, and hour to do vital and urgent administration and an hour in hand for emergencies, then you need to think in terms of five-hour stretches of time. You also need to have a clear idea about what you can achieve in that time and how many units of five hours you will need.

The next thing to do is to break any job down into the tasks:

Reading
Research
Interviews
Writing
Reviewing
Checking

These won't be the same every time, but they broadly correspond to most stages in most writing tasks. If you can make a judgement about the time each of them will take for each job, then you can begin – not just to judge how long it will take overall – but to plan that into your diary well ahead of the deadline.

This needs to be part of the alchemy of writing. Just as editors never reveal their real deadlines to their contributors, it seems to me that freelance writers should avoid revealing their real schedules to their commissioners. It undermines the mystique somehow.

There is one factor, as I hinted above, that can put all that out and lead you to completely misjudge the length of time these things will take: *meetings*. Meetings involve travelling and hanging around and being polite. All are tiring. They are done in the full glare of the client's attention so they can see exactly how long they are taking you. Worse, they often assume that meetings are somehow exempt from the job in hand and won't be paid for.

This often happens when a nervous underling has been put in charge of the job you have been asked to do, and requires constant discussion to reassure them. Worse, you have involved yourself with an old-fashioned charity and the whole committee wants to have constant meetings to see how you are getting on.

It seems to me reasonable that meeting clients to discuss a future job should be done at your own expense. But once the job has begun, all those meetings need to be covered in the budget and accounted for. Better still, you need to be firm with the client and say that you would probably work much more effectively if there was just one meeting at the end to review what you have done and suggest changes, and that you can stay in touch in the meantime by phone.

I argued earlier that the task of a freelance writer is to make friends with their clients, and some meeting is bound to be necessary for that. But constant meetings about specific projects are the bane of our lives as writers and need to be avoided if at all possible. Just say no.

Managing your time

The pioneering psychologist used to talk about the world that might be perceived by a new baby as "blooming, buzzing confusion". That is also what happens if you don't plan your time effectively. It really is rather important.

The trouble with just making a list of things to do and going through it is that in practice it can be deadening, or even depressing. You also don't necessarily prioritise what is most important.

I had two pieces of very good advice which have made an enormous difference to me. The first was to divide everything you need to do into the following categories:

Urgent/important: You need to set time aside at the beginning of every day to do these. They may not take very long, but they do need doing.

Urgent/not important: Do these maybe in the evenings, if there's enough time.

Important/not urgent: These are the key tasks which need to be planned in each day (see below).

Not important/not urgent: Ignore. Life is too short.

This sounds very glib. Life does have a tendency of breaking out of these simple categories, and there may be times when so much is urgent and important that it seems there isn't enough time for anything else. But that may be you are interpreting the word 'urgent' too broadly. If it isn't that, it is the word 'important' which is troublesome. Have a re-think.

Which brings me to the second piece of advice which, as it was explained to me, is about planning your 'elephants'.

How do you eat an elephant? One mouthful at a time, and it makes sense to plan these mouthfuls a month or so ahead. My suggestion is that you split the various tasks in the month ahead into what you can reasonably expect to do in a five-hour day and assign one of them per day. I suggest you keep Fridays free for doing administration like booking train tickets or sending emails or writing follow-ups to emails or bids. Or keeping in touch with clients, of course.

I usually divide book chapters broadly into eight days – four of research and four of writing. These need to be planned ahead and stuck to, if at all possible. The key element is being able to judge how much time you need, which is a serious challenge for me – but then I can't judge the length any journey is going to take, so it is something I need to work on. Otherwise my optimism runs away with me and I end up stressed.

But if you can get this right, your average day (except Fridays) might look something like this:

9am   Start work on the urgent/important tasks.

10am   Stop. Get tea and biscuits ready and start the daily elephant bite.

1pm   Lunch and chill, maybe have a walk.

2pm   More of the daily elephant bite.

5pm   Go home, go out, take a big break.

Later (if time) have a go the other bits and pieces that need doing, especially anything that requires planning for the next day. I find that just reading through the basic task for the morning allows my subconscious to get to grips with it in the night. It is strange how this works, but it seems to.

The central message is this: plan ahead, write lists, and judge the time effectively. Do that and the experience should normally be remarkably stress-free.

V

Dealing with money

Being a writer has a kind of mystique about it. You may actually be a journalist or an editor or any other kind of hack, but the word 'writer' sometimes seems to raise you up above the common herd, like 'actor', as if – just possibly – you might be able to see more deeply than the ordinary mortal. Yet somehow you are expected to deal with the bank, with tax and cashflow and writing invoices and all the rest. It just isn't fair.

It hardly needs saying but the money side of being a freelance writer makes it all possible, or not, as the case may be, and so it has to be dealt with very carefully. There are also a whole range of potential problems to deal with, including your tax status – whether you are employed, self employed or treated as a business yourself for tax purposes. It makes sense to get the advice of an accountant for that. But the biggest problem of all, it seems to me, is the problem of cashflow.

Almost by definition, as a freelance writer, you are not going to be paid regularly. This is the biggest headache for people who write books, as I do. Their lump sum advance payments, if they are lucky enough to get them, will be paid in three stages – when they sign the contract, when they deliver the manuscript and it is cleared for publication, and finally when the book actually comes out. Yet the whole period of thinking about, planning a book and doing enough research to convince a publisher, then getting it commissioned, is paid nothing at all. Worse, the money – such as it is – will need to take you all the way to the next contract, all the way from selling the initial idea to dealing with any feedback and having another idea.

It doesn't work any more. The vast majority of authors won't be able to get by on writing books alone and will need to have other money coming in, but it comes in fitfully sometimes in bursts and sometimes not for months at a time. The worst moment for cashflow is when, every six months, the tax bill arrives and what seems like a huge sum – representing income tax on money earned the previous year – has to be found somehow without financial disaster.

Luckily, I have a magical solution to this, and other problems. It isn't exactly easy, but if you can manage it, this small innovation can smooth out cashflow and provide you with financial cushion like almost nothing else. It is the simple business of opening a tax account.

Tax accounts

I realise what I am asking here, but bear with me. I am asking a new freelance writer, perhaps newly self-employed, who has been struggling for months living on almost nothing and waiting for the first elusive invoice to be paid, to give up a huge chunk of it and put it beyond reach.

That is true – I *am* asking that. But the benefits of doing so are so enormous that it is worth doing, believe me. This is what you need to do:

1. **Open a tax account**. It needs to be a high interest account, if you can find one, but also where the money has to be immediately accessible, so there is a balance to be struck.

2. **Put into the tax account 20 per cent of everything you earn**, without exception. I used to put in a quarter, because income tax was higher when I started, and also because a quarter was easier to work out in my head on the way to the bank than a fifth.

The advantages of this go way beyond having the tax available to pay when you need it. That is not a small advantage in itself. You know that, however large the tax demand is going to be, the money is available in a separate account, earning interest, waiting for the moment that HM Revenue and Customs strikes.

But you also know when those tax demands will come in – at the end of January and the end of July. It means that there is a cushion of money there to borrow from yourself, without having to bother the bank or anyone else who might possibly lend you money, through those drought periods when you are waiting to be paid.

In fact, of course, if you put in 20 per cent of everything you earn, that will almost certainly be more than the tax bill – because there will be expenses to be reclaimed and other payments that you can claim against tax (see below). This means that, in practice, the tax account cushion carries on growing year by year and provides you with vital savings pot for later.

It is extremely important that you only borrow from yourself against invoices that have been sent. You have to be your own factoring service. It is tempting fate to borrow from the tax account just when times are hard, unless it is for those items which might be tax deductable. But there are exceptions to this rule as well. When that elusive invoice finally gets paid, you can then put it the whole thing straight into the tax account and you are all square. This does depend, of course, on your invoice actually *being* paid, otherwise you might be in difficulties.

But of course there will be occasions when you need to borrow larger sums of money from yourself, and the tax account makes this possible. Maybe you need a new fridge or to get married or to pay for or a new bike. It is far cheaper and much less worrying to borrow that money from yourself. If you are self-employed then the tax account is your money until it gets paid over to HMRC (it is different of course if you have set up a limited company which makes the tax account out of reach for anything else).

What I did for more than a decade was that I allowed myself to borrow from the tax account for lump sums in emergency or other circumstances. But the money has to be paid back, so as well as paying 20-25 per cent of each earnings straight into the tax account, you should also as a matter of course pay in another ten per cent.

This has a dual purpose:

• To pay off the money that has been borrowed.

• To build up a nest egg, distributed among various pots in the same account – to cover house repairs, car repairs, holidays, or whatever else requires saving.

This may sound complicated to start with, but it is actually very simple. It means paying up to a third of every bill paid into the tax account and using it as means for ironing out the payment gaps and eventually to managing your own finances. Of course, there is no doubt that it is difficult to start with, when this is the first money that comes in and you have to part with a third of it. But bear in mind that much of that third is owed at some point to the tax man. If you can possibly put it aside, it will save you enormous heartache in the future.

Getting paid

The most important way to get paid is to put in an invoice. It is, in fact, hard to extract the money if you don't. It is all too easy to forget this crucial part of the job, so you need a systematic way of making sure you remember. The best way of doing this is, right from the beginning of the job, to make a note to remind yourself that the invoice must go in once the job is accepted as complete.

It must also go in as soon as possible. Companies can go bust unexpectedly. I have lost a number of fees for just that reason. Any number of other confusions can mess things up if you allow them by delaying. The invoice must go in as soon as the task is finished.

How can you be sure it is finished? There is nothing so irritating as a supplier asking to be paid before they have actually finished the work, so it makes sense to be sure.

Check with your contact in your last conversation – is that it? Do you mind if I send in an invoice? Where should I send it?

The chances are they will say that they just have to run things past their boss or their committee, or past some other peculiar entity you haven't heard of. There always seems to be some last detail that needs to be finished. In which case, call them up or send them a message a week later to find out what happened. If all went well, ask them if it is OK to send in an invoice.

Then in it goes. And if it isn't paid within 30 days, send them a polite note to see if they can follow it up for you. It is important not to let these things drift, as I have discovered the hard way.

There may be some kinds of tasks which get paid automatically. Some appearances on the BBC, for example, or book contracts – though even those tend to need invoices these days. Some newspaper commissions will be paid automatically but extremely late. It is just important to make sure the newspaper accounts department has your email address and your bank details.

For notoriously late payers, and you will soon discover which ones they are – usually the bigger companies, where the accounts department is a million miles from the nice, humane editor you have been working for – it can make sense to put a note on the bottom of the invoice reminding them of the legal position. You are, after all, entitled to claim more money for late payment.

I have personally never actually claimed any money, nor have I ever met anyone who has done it – but that isn't the point. The point is that big bureaucracies occasionally need reminding that there are consequences for their lateness, even if you know, secretly of course, that you will never charge them extra because of the irritating extra work involved.

The phrase which a colleague of mine in the National Union of Journalists uses, and which I occasionally use as well, goes like this:

"I understand and will exercise my statutory right to claim interest and compensation (£40) for debt recovery costs under the late payment legislation if this invoice is not paid according to agreed credit terms (30 days)."

It is simple and a little frightening. Does it work? I don't know, but I am inclined to think that some payments would be even later if I didn't use it at all.

VI

Building a career

I work extremely hard. When I don't have enough work, which is thankfully rare, I work even harder – because I then need ideas for paid work and find I have to act on all of them in case one of them comes off.

I was aware in my forties that I could no longer work quite as I had in my thirties, but then I was a little more established then. People kept coming back for more work for me and I was also writing books. I was aware in my fifties that, again, I would need to shift a little in the way I was working. I had a young family, I could hardly sit in front of my computer all evening as I had done before, and I didn't have quite the enough energy to dash recklessly from meeting to meeting without remembering to have lunch. I could no longer work until the small hours and then fail to get out of bed the next morning until elevenses – which is one of the luxuries, perhaps the besetting sins, of freelance writers.

I also found that, as the decades wore on, that there was a kind of grinding going on in the background as some part of me – without being asked to – began to look for a different way of living and working. Something had to change and, with some pain and difficulty and more than once, eventually it did.

But even if I had felt differently about my levels of energy, I still wanted to develop more of a career. I wanted to be more influential – I know this is embarrassing to confess. I wanted to be, to some extent, the hero of my own life, at least a little more than I was. I wanted a career, the one thing you don't really manage when you are a freelance writer, when nobody tells you how well you are progressing and nobody offers you promotion or the key to the executive washroom. To continue with the David Copperfield analogy, I didn't want to be so Micawberish, just hanging around my entire life for something to turn up.

There were also times when this happened without me quite intending. I was asked in 2012 to carry out an independent review for the Cabinet Office and Treasury on barriers to public service choice. I briefly found myself wearing a suit most days and carrying a civil service security pass, not to mention a battery of codes for a civil service computer. After my report came out the following year, I found that my old clients had changed in their attitudes towards me. Nobody offered me hack editing work any more, as if I was somehow too important now – or so it seemed to me at the time. This was a pity because I could have done with some. But I had to come to terms with the fact that, without me quite asking it to do so, providence had shifted my career.

I have no definitive advice on this problem because I am still working it out myself, but I do have some observations. Here they are.

Writing books

You could fill a whole ebook just about writing books, but there is no doubt this needs to be part of any freelance writer's armoury if they want to develop a career – and especially if they have specialist knowledge or, better still, they are in a position to tell a story which has not been told before (more on this below).

Publishing a book is one of the self-reinforcing proofs of your own expertise and status. It isn't fair, but you only have to do it to prove that you have the expertise you needed to write a book in the first place. The difficulty is that it is extremely time consuming and not very well paid, and – if you are not one of the vast majority of writers who write bestsellers – the potential returns are dropping fast by the day. This is the most innovative period for over a century in publishing, but nobody is really answering the key question: how do we pay the authors?

Part of the problem here is that the economics of publishing has unravelled. There is no place any more for a 'mid-list' and little or no place for an advance. Another part of the problem is that academics need to write books to buttress their position in the research assessment exercise, and they are prepared in effect to pay to do it – and can certainly do it without pay if they have some kind of tenure.

This is an industry that is very much influx, and so is this problem. It seems clear that there is money in the system that could be tapped to pay the authors – just as there is for paying musicians for live performances – if only we can think up ways of extracting it. I have spoken at meetings of 500 people at the Hay Literary Festival, all of whom paid £10 to hear me and the other speakers, but have not received a penny of that money. Something will give and I'm keeping my fingers crossed that it gives during my lifetime.

In the meantime, we have to experiment a little. Ebooks are a whole new market with different rules and different pricing, and different ways of paying the authors too. They are shorter and more informal. There are crowdfunding websites for publishing in various formats. We need to experiment more, rather as Charles Dickens did, with subscriptions to books, and to find new ways of paying for them in the first place as the two markets –

ebooks and beautifully-produced real books – begin to surge apart.

It also makes sense to think about how to write books fast and efficiently, and here is the Boyle Patent Book-Writing Instruction Manual, for those who don't want to agonise for a couple of years to get it down, and to sweat blood from early in the day to late at night while watching all their human relationships unravelling:

1. Decide on a broad structure for the book and a chapter plan and buy small cardboard filing boxes, and label one for each chapter. Everything you come across – notes, articles or anything else – can go in the relevant chapter box until you have time to deal with it at the right time, and without piling up in a disordered, unsortable and stressful way around your desk and floors.

2. Take down the box for Chapter 1 and write notes on everything you want to include in it, including any other books you want to consult or interviews you want to carry out, plus the thoughts you have had about that chapter - and the page references for each quotation you might use for later.

3. You will find that, half way through this process, the structure of the chapter has become pretty clear in your

mind – or at least how to begin and end it, and the stories you will want to include that will bring it alive. So take a break and note it down in as much detail as you can.

4.   Print out the notes for the chapter and put them in some kind of order, as set out in the chapter structure.

5.   Start to write the chapter in as free and as flowing a way as possible from your notes, and when you get stuck - just jump ahead to a place you *do* know what to say or write. Don't go back and correct spelling mistakes or mistypings. Just carry on. And go on like that until the notes have been disposed of (but keep the original computer file so that you can search later for page references and sources).

6.   Go back to the beginning of the chapter and correct it, filling in all the gaps until there is a full flowing draft.

7.   Go through it again.

8.   Repeat for chapters 2, 3, 4 and so on.

9.   When you are half way through the book, you will discover after all what the whole thing is really about, and you will then be free to go back to previous chapters and to alter them accordingly.

10. Print out and read through. Hey presto, you now have a book draft, and the notes with which you can track down the page references relatively easily if it is that kind of book.

This system is designed to prevent waiting around agonising about what to write next. It should also exclude anything like writer's block, though I should also say that it doesn't really work for fiction – which requires a different system, and one which may perhaps be beyond the scope of this book. Everyone's way of writing fiction is so different that I would be hard pressed to distil it.

My personal belief is that we are entering a new model for book production based on shared or self-publishing alliances. At the moment, this is not sophisticated enough to guarantee a good enough shot at a market, but the time will come when it will. All we writers have to do is to stay vigilant, and experiment with new methods until they find something that works for us.

Teaching, speaking and telling stories

I have refrained from giving advice about good writing in this book, partly because seemed a foolhardy thing to do in your own book and partly because I must assume that anyone aspiring to be a freelance writer can do the basic stuff. But I do believe that, for a good freelance writer, the quality of what you write needs to progress.

I suggested this earlier when I urged freelancers to get support or training in creative writing. But there is no doubt that we learned – very slowly in my case – that the most compelling writing is couched in the form of narratives. The most convincing writing, whether it is articles, books, speeches or radio programmes, doesn't just *include* stories, it is knitted together with stories with the very occasional bursts of commentary. That is a tough call and it can take a lifetime to learn how to write dramatic, convincing and compelling prose, often about very ordinary things. But as they say, a journey of a thousand miles starts with a single step – and all you need to do is to stay heading in the right direction.

This is all a way of saying that, as your career progresses, it may turn out to be easier to earn money from more prestigious events, speaking or teaching at some kind of educational institution. The pay is better, and once you have developed the basic speech or basic teaching format, then it is relatively easy to adapt it later. It supports the writing and draws on it – after all, most of our best ideas come from actually thinking them up as we write them down.

Surrendering to fate

It is a peculiar thing, and difficult to describe in a hard-headed book like this one, but when you are self-employed and the master of your own fate, you are paradoxically more aware of the way in which patterns appear to exist in the way that your career develops. Call it probability or providence, call it God, call it luck – I don't know quite what it is – but I have become more aware of the universal forces that seem to shape your experience. Once you have been cast adrift from regular employment, when your fate used to be in the hands of the personnel department, you can see these forces a little more clearly, or at least convince yourself that something else is going on.

Time after time, when I was first freelancing, I went right up to the line without work, only to be offered it out of the blue at the last possible moment, but only when I actually needed it. I found a similar process seemed to be shaping my work when I was editor of a weekly newspaper for half my week, in a process that I knew at the time as 'The Synchronicity Theory of Newspaper Editing' – at least that is what I called it to myself. It means that, when some vital element in the issue drops out at a crucial moment, if you keep calm and wait, then something better will always take its place. You become, in both cases, a little more aware of how the universe abhors a vacuum and moves to fill it.

It is more than that. There is a universal law which, again, I have barely even described to myself, but which nonetheless holds true and it governs freelance writers as much as anyone else. It might make sense to set it out starkly here so that you can judge the truth of it, or otherwise:

If you do the job or the task or the profession that thrills you the most, the money is more likely to come to pay for it.

I can think of no scientific reason why this might be true, and certainly no economic justification, but I have come to believe it. In fact, I see the process at work everywhere.

This implies that I am somehow adept at sitting back and letting providence take over my own career, but actually I have never quite managed just to trust the process. But something happens when we step forth as the heroes of our own lives, cast adrift from in-house pension plans or career paths, and fling ourselves into the hands of coincidence. Why does it get mentioned so little? The only time I have ever seen a process described like this anywhere else, was in a book about mountaineering, W. H. Murray's *The Scottish Himalayan Expedition*. It is a good note on which to end.

"When I said that nothing had been done I erred in one important matter. We had definitely committed ourselves and were halfway out of our ruts. We had put down our passage money— booked a sailing to Bombay. This may sound too simple, but is great in consequence. Until one is committed, there is hesitancy, the chance to draw back, always ineffectiveness. Concerning all acts of initiative (and creation), there is one elementary truth, the ignorance of which kills countless ideas and splendid plans: that the moment one definitely commits oneself, then Providence moves too. All sorts of things occur to help one that would never otherwise have occurred. A whole stream of events issues from the decision, raising in one's favour all manner of unforeseen incidents and meetings and material assistance, which no man could have dreamt would have come his way. I learned a deep respect for one of Goethe's couplets:

'Whatever you can do or dream you can, begin it.
Boldness has genius, power and magic in it!'"

Afterword

I hope you find this short guide useful. It hardly amounts to complete instructions, or a total manual for freelance writing, but it does distil some of the lessons I have learned over the past quarter of a century. Self-employment is like fashion, it seems to me. You get more out of it if you plough your own furrow, and you have to plough your own furrow if you're going to be creative and push forward the boundaries of what is possible. Please let me know if you think I've got it wrong or right, and I will include your comments in a later edition.

Good luck. Thanks for reading it and have a brilliant career....

Other titles by David Boyle

Building Futures

Funny Money: In search of alternative cash

The Sum of our Discontent

The Tyranny of Numbers

The Money Changers

Numbers (with Anita Roddick)

Authenticity: Brands, Fakes, Spin and the Lust for Real Life

Blondel's Song

Leaves the World to Darkness

News from Somewhere (*editor*)

Toward the Setting Sun

The New Economics: A Bigger Picture (with Andrew Simms)

Money Matters: Putting the eco into economics

The Wizard

The Little Money Book

Eminent Corporations (with Andrew Simms)

Voyages of Discovery

The Human Element

On the Eighth Day, God Created Allotments

The Age to Come

What if money grew on trees (*editor*)

Unheard, Unseen: Submarine E14 and the Dardanelles

Broke: How to survive the middle class crisis

Alan Turing: Unlocking the Enigma

Peace on Earth: The Christmas truce of 1914

Jerusalem: England's National Anthem

Give and Take (with Sarah Bird)

People Powered Prosperity (with Tony Greenham)
Rupert Brooke: England's Last Patriot
How to be English
The Piper
Scandal

www.ingramcontent.com/pod-product-compliance
Lightning Source LLC
Chambersburg PA
CBHW060636210326
41520CB00010B/1626